Pwff the B

By David Flin

Dedication:

To the students of Ash Class, Holy Trinity School, who listened attentively during the early stages of the writing.

Thank you for your excellent feedback.

Cover and interior artwork by
Willow Cooke

Contents

Chapter One.
Art for Art's Sake

Pwff was a dragon. Not just any dragon. He was a magic dragon and he lived a long time ago. When he was young, there were knights in armour, and castles, and magicians, and elves.

Pwff was not a big dragon. Not yet. He was about the size of a medium-sized dog. It wasn't easy being a dragon in those days. Knights hunted dragons, looking for the dragon hoard. Elves hunted dragons for sport. Magicians hunted dragons for things to use in their spells.

The big dragons could fight, but Pwff wasn't a big dragon. He had been hatched in London, but he had to leave London when he became too big to pretend to be a goose.

Pwff pretended to be a goose.

He wasn't sure where best to go, but he kept heading west. He told himself that west is best. He spent a lot of time hiding from humans. He had some close calls. He once hid in an oven, and then some woman started baking some cakes. Luckily, she went away, and some man was watching the oven, only he was paying more attention to a book.

Pwff puffed and he puffed and he puffed, sending out his little flames, and he managed to burn a hole in the side of the oven, and he was able to escape. Of course, the cakes were completely burnt, but that wasn't Pwff's problem.

The trouble was, where there was good farmland, there were a lot of farms. Where there were a lot of farms, there were a lot of farmers, who were people. He had to be careful around people. He was, after all, only a small dragon.

Pwff had to hide a lot. Sometimes he had to hide in a hurry. Once he had to hide in a haystack, and he had to hold his breath for ever such a long time. He didn't want to set the haystack on fire. He wasn't a big dragon, so his flames weren't very big, but hay burns easily.

He held his breath, and just as he was about to have to breath, the knight rode out of sight. Once the knight was completely out of sight, and when he was well out of earshot, Pwff leaped out and shouted.

"That's right. You keep on going, you coward. Knights. All the same. You're all cowards." Pwff had, after all, been hatched in London, so he spoke like a Londoner.

"That's right. You run away, Sir Run-Away. Brave knight? Do me a favour."

Then Pwff became aware that he wasn't alone. It was that sensation you get when you know there's someone there without really knowing how you know. Maybe it was through hearing someone breathing, or some sort of awareness, but he realised there was someone close by.

Pwff edged back towards the haystack. He didn't want to let whoever was there know that he was there. He edged backwards, checking to his left and right to see who was there.

Haystacks aren't solid. Pwff knew that there was a problem when he bumped into something solid. It felt like wood. He spun around, and saw that it was an easel, with a part-done painting on it. If there was a painting, then there was someone painting, and the paint was still wet, so whoever was doing the painting was not far away.

Pwff started backing away again. This could be dangerous. He backed away again, and again he bumped into something solid, something hard, like legs. He jumped, and flapped his wings and tried to fly, but there was no updraft he could use to gain height. He squealed.

So did the human, who had backed into him.

"You're a dragon," said the short human. He didn't have a deep voice like the big humans in shells, and he sounded more scared than aggressive.

"Yeah," said Pwff, trying for a mighty roar. "You better watch out, sunshine, or I'll 'ang one on your beak."

"Wait a minute, you're *not* a dragon," said the boy. He was fair-haired, about ten years old, and he was frowning in annoyance.

"I am, too. You're not a knight. You're not wearing a shell."

"I never said that I was a knight. It so happens that I am, but I'm painting, and I don't wear armour while I'm painting. You're too small to be a dragon. *I'm* more of a dragon than you are."

Pwff glowered. He didn't like this baby knight. "Painting? What sort of a knight goes in for painting? *And* you're too small to be a knight. *And* you don't have a sword. You're not a *real* knight."

"I'm painting. I'm not going to use a sword to paint with. That would be silly."

Pwff looked at the painting. It was all squares and circles and shapes and it made no sense to him. "What's this?" he demanded. "It don't look like nuffing."

"What?"

"I said that it don't look like nothing."

"It's not supposed to. It's Art. Art shows the deeper truth."

Pwff looked at it again. Squares and triangles and things that were nearly circles, but not quite round.

"It's 'orrible," he said. "What's that triangle for?" Pwff waved a wing at a blue triangle with a point at the bottom and the base at the top.

"What do you think it is?"

Pwff shrugged. "It's a dragon's face, bursting through some square clouds."

The boy smiled. "Then for you, that's what it is. But you're not a dragon. Dragons are big and fierce."

"I am a dragon."

"Dragons can fly." This was said in a tone that suggested the boy didn't believe Pwff could fly.

"Well, I *can* fly," Pwff snorted.

"Prove it."

"I can't fly here, not today. There ain't no thermals."

The little knight frowned. "What are thermals?"

Pwff looked surprised. "Hot air rises in the air. That's why hot air balloons fly. Air over ground that is warmer gets hotter, and rises. That's a thermal. We use the rising air to get higher. *Everyone* knows that."

The little knight considered this before answering. Then they said: "It's convenient that there aren't any of these thermals here, isn't it. Everyone knows that dragons can fly. You can't fly. Therefore, you're not a dragon."

"We *can* fly, but we need to have thermals so we can get airborne," Pwff explained patiently.

"Right. Dragons can breathe fire. You can't. That means you're not a dragon."

"Yes, I can."

"No, you can't."

Pwff glowered. He wasn't big enough to hold enough fire to burn a knight to ashes, but he could breathe fire. "Watch," he said, and turned his head to one side and roared fire.

He *really* should have looked before he flamed. Everyone knew that you look before you flame, but this knight had made him so angry that he forgot. It was the boy's fault. He was the one who put the easel there. If he hadn't been painting, then the easel wouldn't have been there. But it was, and it was right in the path of Pwff's flame.

He couldn't burn people, but he could burn wood and canvas and paint; the easel caught fire. On its own, that would not have been a problem. What *was* a problem was that the wind blew the flame from the easel into the haystack, which also caught fire.

Oops.

Some farmers saw this and ran towards them to deal with the fire. The farmers were not pleased. Pwff and the boy ran away.

Chapter Two:
And Then There Were Three

Pwff and the boy rested by a river. No-one was chasing them anymore, which was good. They caught their breath, and pretended that they hadn't been running away, because knights and dragons don't run away, especially not from farmers.

"OK, so you can breathe fire, after all" the boy said, grudgingly. "What's your name?"

"I have many names," Pwff explained. "Humans call me Grandeur of the Flaming Skies, while the Elves call me Light of the Night. Dragons call me ..." Pwff then paused. You shouldn't lie about your names, but misleading was expected.

"Dragons call me by my name in our own tongue, which is difficult for humans to master."

"Embarrassing, is it?" The boy was shrewder than he looked.

It's comfortable here.

"Nah. Well, kind of. Maybe. They call me Pwff. Because I've only got a little puff. Pwff means puff. What's your name?"

"I'm Art. I'm going to be a great knight. But I still don't think you're really a dragon." Art and Pwff lay by the river, watching the water go past. It was a sluggish, slow, lazy river, and the water was in no hurry to get to wherever it was going.

The sun shone bright and warm, and little flying, biting insects buzzed around beneath the trees. Pwff wasn't bothered by the insects. He had scales, and the insects couldn't bite through the scales, so they didn't bother him.

They did bother Art, though. They bit him whenever they got a chance, and Pwff thought this must be the reason why humans wore shells.

"I *am* a dragon. I don't think *you're* a boy."

"If you're a dragon, where's your hoard? If you're a dragon, why don't you fly? If you're a dragon, why don't you devastate the countryside?"

Pwff sighed. "I need to *collect* a hoard before I have *got* one. If I fly, well, you can't, and I wouldn't be lying here comfortably. And I *did* devastate the countryside. I burnt down that haystack."

"And then you ran away," said Art.

"You ran away too. I bet you're not a boy."

"That's true, I'm not a boy," said Art. "If I was a boy, I would be at home. Dad said that his first-born would be a son who would grow to be a mighty knight and a great warrior, and a great King. The trouble was, I'm a girl. He then told everyone I was stillborn, born dead, and he tried to kill me, only I got smuggled out. Dad takes his Oaths seriously."

Pwff snorted. "We dragons do it better. Mum lays an egg, puts food nearby, and then leaves it to nature. Strong dragons survive, weak dragons die, and so there aren't any weak dragons."

"What about Dad dragons?"

Pwff snorted, and watched the smoke from his nose form a little spiral column rising into the air. "There aren't any. We switch between male and female. Like seahorses. It's easier."

Art didn't really understand that, so she ignored it. "How do you learn to do things, like flying?"

"I don't know. Dragons just know these things. Dragons don't need to go to school or anything. We just know things."

"I suppose that's why I never saw a dragon when I went to school," Art said.

The two of them lay on the river bank, and together they watched the lazy clouds high above.

"We should go on an adventure."

"It's too comfortable here," said Art.

"Yeah," Pwff agreed. "It's alright here."

"So why did you say we should go on an adventure?"

"That was you, mate," Pwff said. "I'm happy right here."

They continued to lie on the bank and watch the clouds in silence.

"We've been here for too long. Time we went on an adventure."

"No. I don't feel like having any adventures today," said Pwff. Pwff was happy lying there watching the clouds make shapes.

"I agree. No adventures today," Art replied.

"So why did you suggest one, you complete… you complete *human*?"

"I didn't. You did."

"No, I didn't. You did."

"That cloud looks like a horse," Art said.

"No," said Pwff. "Horses have a horn on their head."

"That's unicorns. There aren't many of them around."

"Horses, unicorns. What's the difference? Typical humans. Get other people to do their travelling for you. You're lazy."

"Only girls can ride unicorns, you know," Art said.

Pwff didn't care. The sun was warm, and there was a nice shimmer to everything in the heat. There would be good thermals in the evening, and he could go hunting. In the evening. Not before.

"We should start our adventure."

Pwff was looking at Art, and he could see that she hadn't spoken, and he knew that *he* hadn't. That meant …

Pwff glanced into the tree they were lying beneath. "I think I'll stretch my wings," he said. "I bet you're good at catching things that fall out of trees."

Art looked puzzled, but Pwff had to concentrate on taking off. He extended his wings. He preferred to start from high ground, but this land was boringly flat. He turned to face into the wind, so that the wind blew into his leathery wings, so that they could act like a sail. He looked around to see where the rising thermals were.

There was a good patch over an outcrop of rock, so he would aim for that, and then let the updraft give him altitude.

"What are you waiting for?" Art asked, getting impatient.

"Take-off and landing are the most dangerous parts of flying. You've got to get them right."

Pwff looked again, and he concentrated. Dragons aren't built for running, which is why they prefer to only fly on windy days.

"Go on, then," said Art.

Pwff glowered. He wanted to say something, but he would need all his puff for this take-off. He straightened out his tail so that it didn't get caught up in his legs. It's *really* embarrassing when you trip over your tail during take-off. Wings angled just right. Check the running way for obstacles. Lift your tail into the air so that its weight is pushing you forward.

And then run like hell, feeling the pressure of the wind on your wings, and when you can't run any faster, you jump forward into the air, spread your wings as wide as you can, flap once, twice, three times to get some height, and then lean into the corner to head for the thermal.

Then feel the rising air, and spread your wings wide to catch every last bit of the thermal, and circle within it, rising as the air rose, up, and up, and up.

Pwff was high, high up in the sky. Dragons don't really fly; they glide. But when you can get a good thermal, you can get ever so high, and Pwff was now ever so high.

So high that he had to blink and adjust the muscles of his eyes so that he had his flying eyes. Dragon's eyes have lots of different muscles, and by tensing some muscles and relaxing others, they can see either close things or far-off things. Up here, he needed to see far-off things.

There were mountains far off to the west, and desolate moorland to the southwest.

Beneath him, a thousand metres below, there was the river and the trees and Art. There was a bird in one of the trees. A bird of prey, some sort of eagle, only eagles don't live here.

Most dragons don't like steep dives, but Pwff did. Speed was a thrill, but if you got it wrong in a steep dive, well, you hit the ground at a speed that would leave bits of dragon scattered for miles around.

"Which is why you mustn't get it wrong," Pwff said to himself. He lifted his tail up so that his head pointed downwards, and he tucked his wings in close to his body, and gravity took over. Slowly at first, but then faster and faster; the ground came rushing up towards him. He switched to his close-range eyes as the ground came closer, and twisted so that he pointed right at the tree with the eagle in it.

Then he spread his wings and breathed fire to create a small thermal, and levelled out in a rush of wind and flapping wings.

The tree caught fire, the eagle jumped out, and Art caught it and held it.

Got you.

"Let me go, you barbarian," said the eagle, wriggling furiously.

"Why?" Art asked it. "You were spying on us. Who are you spying for? Who is your magician, foul familiar?"

Pwff landed nearby, and waddled over to help Art. He had heard about magicians, and how they butchered dragons for ingredients for spell recipes. Eye of dragon and dragon's heart and all the rest. Pwff decided that he didn't like magicians. He took a deep breath, and prepared to flame the familiar.

"Don't!" shouted Art and the eagle at the same time.

"You'll burn me," Art added.

Pwff couldn't stop the flame, but he was able to turn his head just in time. The flame hit the river, and boiled away a lot of the water, and a fish flopped out onto the bank, boiled and cooked and ready to eat.

"I don't like eagles," said Pwff.

"I'm not an eagle," said the bird.

"Don't be daft. You're an eagle. I can *see* you're an eagle," said Pwff.

"It's not an eagle," said Art. It's a merlin. That's a type of small falcon."

"Unhand me, you oaf. I'm not a merlin."

"If you're not an eagle," said Pwff.

"And if you're not a merlin," added Art, "then what are you?"

The merlin gave a deep sigh, and its body shimmered and shifted, wings becoming arms, face becoming human, feathers becoming clothes. After a moment, Art found he was holding a boy.

"OK," said Art, trying to pretend that birds turning into boys was a common thing, and nothing unusual.

"Are you a bird or a human?" Pwff asked.

"Neither," the boy replied. "I'm a shapeshifter."

"I know about shapeshifters," said Art excitedly. "When you kill them, they turn into what they really are."

"What I will turn into, barbarian, is dead. When I die, all of the pent-up magic inside me is released at once, and it will devastate the countryside for miles around."

Pwff laughed. "I can devastate the countryside, and he can devastate the countryside. What can you do, Art?" Pwff poked his tongue out at Art, and dragons have a lot of tongue they can poke out. He waved his tongue around to emphasis his words.

"I will be a King and I will rule the countryside wisely," Art said.

"What fun is that?"

"It's duty. Duty isn't supposed to be fun. Why didn't you fly away?" Art asked the shapeshifter.

"I can change into the form of animals. I don't get their abilities."

"What use is that?"

"Knowledge is power. I hear lots of things, I gain knowledge, and so I gain power. I have a Destiny," the shapeshifter added proudly.

"Another person with a Destiny? What's your destiny?" Pwff asked.

"Not got a clue, old fellow, not got a clue," he said. "I've got one, though."

"What's your name?" Art asked.

"No idea."

"We shall call you Merlin, because you were a merlin when we met you. I also have a Destiny. I will be a Great King, and I believe that you and Pwff are to be a part of that."

"You can't be a king," said Merlin. "You're a girl."

"I can."

"No, you can't. It's against the Rules."

Art considered this carefully. "Very well. Together, we will break the Rules. It's a silly rule, and I'm only going to have wise rules when I'm a wise ruler."

Chapter Three
Morgan You Bargained For

Pwff, Art and Merlin argued a lot about which way they should go. Pwff wanted to head towards the mountains. Flying was better and easier there. Art kept saying that the moorland was where they should go.

As for Merlin, whatever either Art or Pwff said, Merlin said that they were wrong. Pwff thought that Merlin just enjoyed arguing. They couldn't agree, so Merlin suggested leaving it to Destiny to decide.

"Destiny is a coin?" Art asked.

"An impartial arbiter when points on both sides are valid. Fate decides our courses when we are in a balanced position. The wise ruler always consults fate in this way before making a decision."

Art didn't seem convinced. "I will not let a coin make decisions for me."

"I don't see why not. It's got just as much brains as you have."

They argued some more about it and, eventually, Art agreed to see what the coin said.

"Heads means we head towards the mountains; tails towards the moors," said Art, tossing a coin high in the air. The three of them watched it spin, and then land on the ground.

The three gathered around the coin, looked at it, and Art shouted in joy. "Tails! That means we're off to see the moorland." Art crowed in triumph. "It is our destiny to go to the moors. We'll see the Dancing Stones and the Never-Ending Hole and the Golden Bow and the Invisible Castle."

Merlin sniffed. "And how, oh wise ruler-to-be, will we see the Invisible Castle? It's invisible."

"And we're going to see it," Art said cheerfully.

Pwff flicked out his tongue and picked up the fallen coin. He was a bit disappointed that he'd lost the toss, but on the plus side, he now had the coin. He had made a start on gathering his treasure hoard. All dragons need a dragon hoard, after all.

It's mine now.

*****

They reached the edge of a wood, and the clouds grew very dark. Pwff could tell that it was going to rain soon, and dragons don't like being out in the rain. Rain reduces thermals, and it makes flaming difficult, and it gets in the eyes.

The trees were dark and bent and twisted, like gnarled bushes. Mainly thorn trees, and the branches were covered with long, thin spikes. It was hard for Merlin and Art to walk between the trees without getting scratched. Pwff chortled. His scales had grown thick enough that the thorns didn't bother him.

They rested beneath the trees, and Merlin entertained them by turning into different animals and seeing whether Pwff or Art could guess what animal he was.

"Can you shapeshift into the King?" Art asked.

"No," Merlin explained. "I can only shapeshift into a type of animal, not a specific one. A horse is not a problem. Bucephalus, no, I can't do that. That's a specific horse."

"Who's Bucephalus?" Pwff asked.

"A famous horse," Art answered. She made it sound like it was obvious. She wasn't sure of the details, though.

"Bucephalus was the horse owned by Alexander the Great," came a voice from among the trees.

"I thought so," said Merlin. "These are the famous talking trees of Birnam Wood."

Pwff frowned. He'd seen a play about that. "They were walking trees, not talking trees."

"You can't walk without talking," Merlin explained.

"Yes, you can," Art answered.

"*You* can't. Jabber, jabber, the whole way. If you couldn't speak, you'd be immobile. Yes, this is the walking, talking Birnam Wood."

"Isn't Birnam Wood in Scotland?" Pwff was puzzled.

"It *was* in Scotland. They're *walking* trees." Merlin sounded really exasperated.

"It's not the trees talking," said one of the trees.

"It's the trees," Merlin said confidently. "They're scared of Pwff, because trees burn."

"It's not the trees," said Art. "It's the bandits hiding among the trees."

"How can you tell?" Pwff asked. He had no sooner finished speaking when an arrow flew from the shadows within the wood and into the ground inches in front of Art.

"The walking, talking trees of Bowman Wood. Birnam is another word for Bowman," Merlin said quickly.

"Who are you?" Art called out.

"*You* come into *my* wood, without so much as a by-your-leave, and now *you* want to know who *I* am?" The voice was that of a girl, surprisingly soft and melodious.

The bow is loaded.

"Well, yes," said Art. "You see, it was Destiny that brought us here, so Destiny intended for us to meet, so we need to introduce ourselves. I am Art, and I am destined to be a Great King. This idiot chatterbox is Merlin, my wise advisor, and this is Pwff, a dragon who will have a great lineage in the future. He, actually, Pwff, what do you *do*?"

"I look after the money," said Pwff, without thinking. He suddenly thought that this might have been a mistake when he saw an arrow pointing directly at him.

"Who are you?" Art asked into the shadows.

"I am an outcast. Half-elf, half-mortal, accepted by neither. These are my woods, and strangers enter at their own peril."

"That's all right," said Pwff. "We're not strangers. We've been introduced. Besides, we're outcasts too, so you could join us and share in Art's Destiny."

"Why should I?"

"Because there are mysteries that will be revealed in the course of our adventures," said Merlin.

There was an uncomfortable silence in the shadows.

"Because obviously our coming here means our fates are entwined," said Art.

There was an uncomfortable silence in the shadows.

Pwff shook his head. Stupid people. They really didn't understand outcasts. "Because the mortals will hate it if you join us, and you'll really annoy them. The elves will also hate it if you join us. That means you'll upset them both. It will be fun." Besides, thought Pwff, it would be nice if that arrow wasn't pointed at him.

There was a lengthy silence, and then a dark-haired girl stepped into the clearing. She was, well, Pwff wasn't good at judging age, but she was a bit taller than Art, but not as stocky. She wore dark brown, mottled clothes, and held a bow in her hands. Still loaded, Pwff noted uncomfortably. She moved without making a sound. Pwff noticed that her eyes were like those of a cat, and were black in colour.

"Fun?" she asked, raising an eyebrow. "That could be fun. I am Morgan. Morgan of the Fey, only the Fey don't want me.

*****

Pwff wondered why Morgan seemed to have been happy in this wood of thorn trees. It was lonely, dark, and gloomy. He asked her.

"Because it's lonely, dark, and gloomy," she told him.

Pwff was puzzled by this. It seemed very odd.

Morgan sighed. "Lonely is good because that means you don't have anyone bothering you. Gloomy is good, because that depresses your enemies. Dark is good, because when it is dark, the prey can't see you coming."

"Oh." Pwff preferred the day. Thermals were better during the day, and it was usually cold at night. "Do you have any *actual* enemies?"

Morgan mumbled something.

"What?" Pwff asked.

"Not yet, OK. Not real enemies. But I will."

"You *want* enemies?"

"How can you be victorious over your enemies if you don't have any enemies?" Morgan sounded puzzled.

Pwff didn't understand this. "But what if the enemies are victorious over you?"

"I don't understand," Morgan replied. "That would mean that *I* lost to *them*. I'm not sure that's possible."

"Of course it's possible. Haven't you ever lost?" Pwff knew that dragons often lost, usually when they'd been quietly playing with some princess and then a stupid knight came along who didn't understand the game.

"I've had setbacks. But humans are impatient and get old and die, and they have no conception of magic.

Elves can't withstand iron. How can I lose?"

Art had heard, and came over. "You understand magic?" she asked.

"I was born in an elf-hill. Of course I understand magic. I know the first magic. Well, some of it."

"What is the first magic?" asked Art.

"Are you an elf-born?" Morgan asked.

"No."

"Then you won't understand. What's your destiny?"

"Are you a mortal-born?" asked Art.

"My father was a mortal. He was a vile, deceitful, angry man. All I know of him is that he does not know of my existence."

Pwff scratched his head. If she didn't know anything about him, then how did she know that he was a vile, deceitful, angry man?

Art didn't notice this little logical problem. "My father tried to kill me," she said.

"Well, my father didn't care about me enough to try."

"My father is a great knight," Art said.

Morgan shrugged. "So's my father. Great knights aren't that great."

"What's a father?" Pwff asked. "Dragons don't have fathers. If a dragon decides to lay an egg, we make ourselves female, and lay an egg."

"What do you mean by that, make yourself female?" Art was puzzled.

"Sometimes we're male and sometimes we're female. It depends on what we feel like being."

Morgan and Art agreed that this was weird.

"I say, chaps," Merlin called. "I've worked out where our Destiny lies. We need to seek out the Castle Beyond the Night."

"Which night?" Morgan asked.

Art started laughing loudly. "You said which night. That's funny."

Morgan glared at Art. "Why is it so funny?"

"You know the first magic, so that means you're a witch. You also carry weapons, so that means you're a knight. Witch knight, which night. Which night, witch knight."

46

Pwff sighed, smoke coming out of his nostrils. This was going to be a long trip.

Chapter Four.

It's trudge, trudge, trudge.

Pwff was right. It had been a long trip. Both Art and Morgan had constantly exchanged barbs about each other, and in between those they exchanged increasingly bad jokes about witch knight. Merlin was no help. He said it was easier to walk as a horse, so he turned into a horse.

That would have been fine, but every so often, he'd decide to be a different sort of horse, or a different colour. That would have been fine, but every time they passed some horses, he would hurry over, and shift to be a similar sort. Then he would hide, and see how long it took the others to find him.

On their way.

It was all very annoying. Pwff suspected that Merlin knew that, and was doing it deliberately. He stopped doing it when Art told him to stop talking. "You can't talk if you're a little horse. You know, a little hoarse."

The countryside became hillier and more desolate. Trees and fields gave way to moorland and marsh. Mist filled the valleys, and the streams and brooks cut deeply into the ground as the water darted towards the sea. The sun struggled to break through the low-lying cloud, and it was hard to see in any direction. The air sat heavy, without a breath of wind.

It was poor flying weather. Pwff wondered if they were just walking round and round in circles, but he supposed that the fact that the ground was different meant that they weren't.

His feet hurt. He didn't like walking. If dragons were meant to walk, they wouldn't have wings. They certainly wouldn't have tails. Tails were great in the air. You could steer using your tail. It got in the way when you're walking, and sometimes getting caught between your legs, and it sometimes getting caught in things on the ground. Pwff hated walking.

"Carry me," he asked Art.

"You're a dragon. Knights don't carry dragons. Dragons are huge and dangerous."

"I'm tired. Are we nearly there yet?" Pwff asked.

"It's about ten miles to go," said Morgan.

"How do you know?" Art asked. "We can't see anything much because of this mist."

"Because of the power," Morgan said, as though that explained every-thing. She didn't seem inclined to say anything more, even when Art asked her.

The four of them walked in silence for a few steps.

"Is it nine miles now?" Pwff asked. "We must be nearly there now."

"Magic is based on power," Merlin explained. "It is possible to use your own power to perform feats of magic, but that never ends well."

"Why not?" Pwff didn't really understand magic.

Merlin grabbed at the chance to explain. "It's because magic involves spending power. If the magic you spend is your own power, then that is gone. Use too much, and you kill yourself. Even using a little weakens you forever. That's why using magic first involves gathering the power you need."

"Thanks," Art said. She thought Merlin had finished.

"Now," Merlin continued, "there is power everywhere. In some places, there is not a lot of it, and drawing on the power is a lengthy process, and any magic that uses it is weak. In other places, called places of Power, there is a lot, and it is quick and easy to use it, and this magic is much more powerful."

"That's why they call it a Place of Power, I suppose," Art said. "It's a place where there's a lot of Power. Thanks."

"Practitioners of the First Magic are able to sense concentrations of magic in different places, in the same way that dragons can sense thermal in different places," Merlin continued.

"Thanks," Art said, firmly. "That means shut up. I've got the gist. No, we're not there yet, Pwff."

Pwff closed his mouth. He had indeed been about to ask if they were nearly there yet, and he wondered how

Art knew that was what he was about to ask.

The four of them trudged on in silence. It was cold, and dragons don't like the cold. A breeze started to blow, and the mist started to clear.

"Of course," Merlin said, "it's possible to use the power from someone else, but that's not a good thing to do."

"We *must* be nearly there," said Pwff.

As he spoke, the wind blew away just enough mist that they could see a bit further.

They were on a meandering track through what looked like red-topped hills. There were a few sheep on the hill slopes, and Pwff felt his stomachs start to rumble. He probably couldn't eat a whole one, but they looked tasty.

Ahead, they could see that the track was winding its way towards the sea, and they could just about hear the sounds of the waves. Then a puff of wind blew some more mist away, and they could see a castle standing on an island outcrop of rock, connected to the mainland by a narrow stone bridge. The edge of the land ended in a cliif, with a sharp drop nearly one hundred feet to the sea below.

On the mainland side of the stone bridge was a low wall, separating the bridge and around 20 feet of cliff edge from the rest of the mainland.

The castle was old, they could all see that, even from this distance. It looked deserted.

It wasn't a fairy castle, all spires reaching towards the sky, looking fragile. It wasn't a castle that was essentially a large house with thick walls. It wasn't a small castle, like a toy. It was a castle that sat on the rocks and glowered at the world, telling the world that it was here to do a job, and that job was to protect people inside the castle.

Glowering at the world.

Enduring. That was the word to describe it.

"Why," Art wondered, "does the castle have two gateways? There's one to the bridge, and there's one next to it, going to nowhere. Why?"

"Built by dwarves," said Merlin. "They called it Kastali til bjod utan nett. That means Castle Beyond the Night."

"We're nearly there!" said Pwff, happily.

Chapter Five.
A Place of Power.

They decided that it was their Destiny to take a closer look at the castle. As they reached the wall on the mainland, Pwff could feel a tingling on his scales. He saw that the others had noticed this. It felt like the air just before a thunderstorm, but there was no thunderstorm coming.

"What is it?" he asked. "Is this a Place of Power?"

"No," said Morgan. The pupils of her eyes were narrow slits, and she had carefully put away her weapons. Little coloured sparks of fire darted from one fingertip to another. "This one has a mind."

"Friend or foe?" Art asked.

"You'll not need your sword," Morgan said.

"They're friends?"

"No," said Morgan. "It's just that it won't do any good."

Magic flooding the area.

They reached the wall and then stopped. There was no grass at all beyond the wall, and a deep sense of foreboding that came from the castle hang heavily in the air. None of them wanted to be the first to suggest they leave, and none of them wanted to be the first to cross into the forbidden area.

Morgan looked at the sparks flickering along the ground, looking like dancing fireflies. The air inside the castle shimmered like it does on a hot day, although it wasn't that hot. "There's magic flooding out there," she said. "I'll be filled with it. Too much of it, and I'll explode."

"Pwff, can't you fly above it and see what's there?" Art asked.

"What is there to see?" Merlin responded. "There's no life there, and there is a lot of magic, and the magic is saying: 'Go away'. We would do better to send a sheep across the bridge, but the sheep will have the sense not to go."

"What's the worst that can happen to us if we take a little look?" Pwff wondered.

Morgan considered this. "Those of us who have souls could have them sundered from the body, making them immortal."

That didn't sound too bad, Pwff thought.

"Then," Morgan continued, "we could be plunged in the nether realms, and then tortured unceasingly for all eternity."

"Let's not do that," Pwff said.

The four of them looked at the castle, hesitant. Then Art's face took on a determined look.

"That's where our Destiny lies," she said.

"Let's not just rush in," Pwff said. "I've kind of got an idea."

"What do you know about magic, wyrm?" Merlin snapped.

"Nuffin'", Pwff said, his voice slipping back into a London accent. But I can see everything in that castle is pointing at the bridge. Let's not use the bridge."

"Unless it has escaped your notice, the only way to get there on foot is across that bridge. Unless it has escaped your notice, three of us can't fly. Unless it has excaped your notice, you're too small to carry anyone, never mind *all* of us." Art could be *really* sarcastic at times.

Merlin could be saracastic as well. "Oh, mighty King-to-be. Unless it has escaped your notice, Morgan is kind of full of magic and needs to use it up. If she doesn't use it up, she'll, well, she needs to use it up. So, small dragon becomes big dragon."

"That's second magic," Morgan replied.

"That's if you're bound by the rules of the elves. It applies in the Summer Country. Not here. You are neither elf nor mortal. You are bound by no rules of elf or human You make your own rules." Merlin spoke with an unctuous, persuasive tone.

"Can you do it?" Art asked.

"No," Morgan said. She was crackling with little sparks; her hair was standing on end.

"Yes, you can," Pwff shouted. "Merlin shapeshifts. He changes size. A horse is bigger than an eagle, so he changes size when he changes shape. Just copy that." Pwff rather liked the idea of being a large and mighty dragon.

Morgan steepled her fingers in thought. As she did so, sparks flew between them, crackling and popping and fizzing as they did so. Her hair was glowing and shimmering. Her clothes waved in the breeze, although there was no wind blowing.

"I need to do *something* to get rid of some of this magic," Morgan said, sounding strange. Was she worried? Pained? Something like that.

Pwff closed his eyes. He wasn't sure that he wanted magic cast on him, although he did want to be a big and mighty dragon that could terrorise pirates and bandits and giants. He woundered if having magic cast on him would hurt. He was certain that it would.

The tingling in his scales grew intense. It was like having an itch all over, and he flicked his tail to try and scratch between his wings, where the itching was worst. His tail brushed against something, and he was then able to scratch, and he gave a big sigh of relief.

"Open your eyes," said Art. "And stop waving your tail around. You'll hurt someone."

Pwff wondered why Art was so close to the ground. Her voice was coming from way down, rather than being way above his head as it usually was.

Pwff cautiously opened an eye. The castle was still there, although it seemed to have hunkered down even more, and it looked cross. It looked angry. He looked at the wall, and

something had happened to it. A part
of it had been knocked over.

Fully grown.

Then he looked at the others, and
they seemed really small. He stood up,
and the ground looked a long way
away, and the boulders of the wall

were just little pebbles. He stretched his wings, and felt that he could do *anything*.

"Pwff?" Art said, awe in her voice. "Are you all right?"

"Oh yes," Pwff said. His voice sounded like a boom. "Come on, what are we waiting for?"

Morgan spoke to Art. "Of course he's all right. That's just what he'll be like when he's fully grown."

Pwff looked at the three. "Come on," he said. "I'm *hungry*."

Chapter Six.
The Castle Beyond the Night

They had managed to fit on his back. There wasn't a great deal of room, but Merlin had changed into a spider, so only Art and Morgan took up room. He would have to be careful, because if they couldn't hold on, they'd fall, and that would probably hurt them.

He didn't have far to fly, so he didn't have to gain a great deal of height.

He didn't *have* to, but there was a wonderful updraft at the cliff's edge, one that was just meant for riding, and Pwff was keen to try out this new big body that he had. He stretched his wings wide, and he felt the air pushing him upwards. He wanted to see how high his big wings would take him.

He looked down, and he was surprised at what he saw. Far, far beneath him, he could see the cliff edge where it met the sea. Waves splashed angrily against the hard cliff, but the sound of its pounding was a distant, far-off murmur. He had never been this high before, and he had to switch to his long-range eyes.

He looked inland, and he saw that there were no farms, just a few scattered buildings where shepherds lived, and a few sheep were munching disconsolately on a few patches of rough grass.

His stomachs started to rumble, and he turned to face these sheep. He knew that the collective noun for sheep was not, as humans thought, a flock, but a snack. That looked like a very tasty snack of sheep.

"Pwff, the castle," Art shouted in his ear. "Castle first. Play later."

Pwff looked longingly at the sheep, and he considered dropping the people that were on his back into the sea. He wasn't a pet, nor was he a servant. He wasn't an animal working for a master. He was a *dragon*.

"Come on, Pwff. We're friends."

Did dragons have friends? Pwff wasn't sure about that. "I'm hungry," he said.

"There may be sheep on those hills, but there may be great food in the castle store. And gold."

Gold. Pwff liked the sound of that word. And the sheep weren't going to go very far away. He turned his head towards the castle.

Pwff looked for somewhere inside the castle that was large enough for him to land. He didn't really know how much space that he would need now that he was a big dragon. He suspected that he was about to find out the hard way.

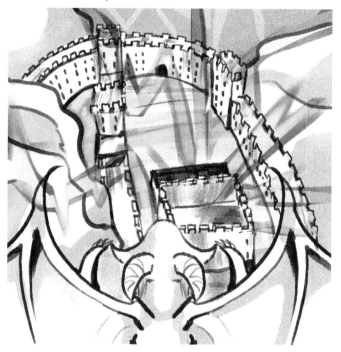

Looking for a place to land.

Each corner of the large keep at the seaward end of the castle had a solid tower. There was a large courtyard between the keep and the landward walls. The courtyard was overgrown and in disrepair, but the walls looked solid enough.

There wasn't a breath of wind. That was going to make landing straightforward. He could just pick whatever path he liked, and not worry about whether or not he was heading into the wind.

He wondered how high he was. Then he remembered hearing echoes when he was playing in the streets of London. He roared at the sea far below. Nothing happened for some seconds, but then he heard the echo of his roar. He tried again, and this time counted in his head. He had reached nine when he heard the echo. That meant that they were at a height of nine.

"So much for the element of surprise," he heard Merlin mutter.

Pwff snorted in disgust. Dragons don't sneak up and surprise people.

"Hold on tight," he shouted. He stretched out his wings so that he could glide. Then he carefully adjusted the angle of his wings to change his height and speed, and come down fast.

He wasn't used to being this big. Maybe he shouldn't come in *this* fast, he thought as he passed the outermost wall. He twisted his wings like a sail, so that he could slow himself down, but he *really* wasn't used to being this big, and one side slowed faster than the other.

Pwff wondered briefly if something *could* slow down faster.

Surely, if it was faster, it wasn't slowing down? He wondered about this as his right claw touched the ground, and he dug it in to the earth to try and slow down before crashing into the far wall. His right side slowed down more than his left, and he spun sideways on to the wall. He sprayed earth and dirt and pebbles as his claw gripped, and his tail swung around uncontrollably, flattening an old wooden shack. Possibly stables.

Then he crashed side-on against the far wall, knocking a few stone blocks out. The others tumbled off of his back, Art landing on her feet, and Morgan and Merlin sprawled in the dirt, getting up quickly.

Crash landing.

It had once been a nice courtyard, with trees and paving stones and overlooked by large balconies from the keep. However, it was all old and uncared for. The paving stones were tilted and cracked, bushes and undergrowth had run rampant, the wooden doors had rotted away.

There were two open gateways. Pwff looked through one, and could see the bridge leading to the moorland, where they had come from. He looked through the other, expecting to see it leading nowhere. He was wrong. He saw that the bridge led to a verdant grassland.

That was puzzling, but he had other concerns. The air fizzed and popped with power, and Morgan was crackling and shining brightly, a bright glow surrounding her. Pwff could sense that there was a lot of magic here. He could also smell Morgan's hair starting to smoulder and burn.

"This is going to get bad," Merlin muttered, shifting himself into a large, grey creature, with thick, solid legs, bigger even than the biggest horse. He had a solid, heavy horn on his head.

"Is that a unicorn?" Art asked.

"Oaf," said Merlin. "I'm a rhinuse, a rhonescu, a rhinokose ... I'm an *African* unicorn." Merlin looked around with his small eyes, and shook his head. "This is not good. Something bad will hap..."

Chapter Seven.
The Round Table

Before Merlin had finished speaking, a shimmering light appeared in the air between them and the keep, and things started to solidify within the swirling air.

"Perhaps they'll be friendly?" Merlin said, hopefully and not believing a word. All four of them could feel waves of hatred and anger emanating from the shimmering, and the things started to step forward into the courtyard. They were goblins, lots of them.

"I'm not going to say anything else," Merlin said.

"Thank you," said Art. "I think we've already got enough problems."

She should have known better. An ogre, 10 foot tall and covered in thick scales that might have been armour or might have been skin stepped forward, brandishing a large wooden club.

Pwff hunched his shoulders, and prepared to launch himself at the ogre.

"No," said Art. "You handle the goblins. I'll handle the ogre. Morgan, this is all being powered by the magic here, you need to get rid of it. Merlin, the magic must be coming from somewhere. Find a way to stop it."

Pwff glowered. He was big enough to handle an ogre.

"Yes," Art said, seeming to read his mind. "But you've got lots of ways of knocking enemies down; claws, teeth, tail, wings. I've got one, my sword. I will handle one enemy, you can handle lots."

I'll handle the ogre.

Pwff bristled, but Art had a point. He'd deal with the goblins, and then he'd deal with the ogre. He roared as loud as he could at the goblins, and as he did so, he wondered why he had followed Art's instructions. What she said might have made sense, but Pwff hadn't even thought about that, he just did what Art had said.

His roar scared the goblins, and they stopped, glancing at each other, claws clicking uneasily. The goblins were tiny, about the size of Art, with big white eyes, and long, straggly hair. They couldn't run away back into the shimmering, because more of them were pushing forward from behind.

Then Pwff ploughed into them. His tail swung and knocked some over; he flapped his wings, knocking others over, and he roared and bit and stamped and swung, and though he knocked over many goblins, more leapt onto him and tried to claw at him with their sharp, long nails. They kept trying to tear some of his scales off so that they could tear at him. He crashed against walls to knock them off.

Out of the corner of his eye, he saw the ogre smash its club down at Art, but she stepped out of the way, and tried to cut at its wrist with her sword. Then Art caught her feet on a fallen goblin, and stumbled, and the ogre swung its club again.

Pwff flicked his tail, hitting the ogre's legs and knocking it over. Then he had to concentrate on all these little goblins. He could scatter them like twigs, but there were always more of them.

He could sense Morgan syphoning off magic from the air, and using it as fast as she could, but there was always more magic keeping the portal open. The magic was flooding in faster than Morgan could dispose of it. Art's sword was glowing and sparking, and its brightness left after-images in the air as she swung it. The ogre wasn't getting tired, despite wielding the huge club.

Merlin, as an African unicorn, charged into the keep, knocking over the goblins that got in his way, and then he fled away from the fight.

Pwff snarled. The coward. Then he had other worries. The goblins were trying to lassoo him and tie him down, and he rampaged wildly. He dragged the ropes and pulled the hordes of goblins along as they tried to hold on; he roared and rolled, and swung his tail. Blocks of stone flew from the walls when he rolled into them.

As the rocks fell, they stopped in mid-air, glowing with magic, and then flew into clumps of goblins. One hit the ogre on the back of his head, and it roared, distracted from Art for a moment, and then started to make for Morgan.

Art saw her chance, and stabbed at the ogre's foot, pinning the foot to the ground. The ogre stumbled and fell with a crash, jerking Art's sword out of her grasp. Pwff tried to swing his tail to bash the ogre, but found he couldn't move it. The goblins had thrown enough ropes to tie it down. Pwff roared, and breathed.

Before, his flames had always been small and not very hot. He wasn't used to the flames of a mighty dragon, and a huge gout of flame scorched across the courtyard like a furnace. The old dry timbers and rotting wood nearby suddenly burst into flame.

Then, from within the keep came the sound of a great crash, and the biggest monkey Pwff had ever seen stood in the doorway of the keep, holding an enormous circle of wood above its head. Then it spoke. It was Merlin.

"Don't stare at me," he said. "It's just everyday gorrila warfare." With that, he bounded to the centre of the shimmering, and slammed the wood on the floor.

Pwff pulled and twisted, and his tail came free, although the ropes were still wrapped around him, and dozens of goblins held desperately onto the ropes, being swung in all directions as Pwff swished his tail.

Then, all of a sudden, there were no goblins and no ogre. Pwff could feel the scratches and the bruises, and the fires were still burning. The fires weren't normal fires, though. They leaped with malignancy at anything that could burn; they swayed and whispered angrily, they sparked and dived towards anyone who came near them. The fire fizzed and spat and burned hotter than it had any right to burn.

The magic was angry. It was throwing the fire where it would hurt and do the most harm. Pwff hadn't realised that magic had emotions, but this magic did; it was angry and it wanted to hurt things.

"There's still too much magic," Morgan said, sounding desperate. She was glowing, and Pwff thought he could see through her.

"Use it up," Art replied.

"How?" Morgan pleaded. She was sounding desparate.

"I don't know," Art said. "Make the castle nice."

Morgan had a scowl on her face "This will not be easy," she muttered. She started to chant, holding her hands straight out in front of her, fingers moving, shifting and squeezing the air as though she was kneading dough to make bread. Sparks flew between her fingers; in the courtyard, bushes and small trees hauled themselves out of the ground, roots and all, and broke themselves into convenient firewood size, and stacked themselves up into neat piles. Then blocks of stone started shifting and rubbing against each other, sanding themselves to fit snugly, before flying to fit the holes in the walls where Pwff had bumped.

Broken paving stones fitted back together and moved back into position, and the largest trees sprang out of the ground to clear room.

The first tree trunk exploded in a shower of green and blue sparks and splinters. Morgan groaned with effort, and her chanting took on a slightly different tone. The next tree trunk shivered and fell into planks; a surge of heat cooked the sap out of them. Then another plank and another.

Making the castle nice with magic.

Pwff felt the magic in the air crackling and fighting and sparking, and Morgan still seemed to be glowing. Her hair looked like it was on fire; it wasn't, but it swirled, and sparked, and her black hair looked like glowing coal.

Morgan started to draw the magic away, and you can't stop until the magic has been drained. However, Pwff wasn't sure what would happen if Morgan couldn't get rid of the magic quickly enough. He guessed that it wouldn't be good.

Morgan looked at the two gates hanging from their hinges. The wood of the hinges flared up in a flash of heat and light, and then the planks of thick wood that she had built up flew into position. Crosspieces slammed against the standing planks, and bolts hurled themselves like arrows to pierce both the upright planks and the crosspieces. Nuts leaped from the ground and whirred into place. The hinges clanked into position, and the gates hang properly once again.

Magic still crackled in the air, and fires still burned in the courtyard. Morgan looked upwards, and pointed at a cloud. A lightnining bolt sprang from her fingers, forking and splitting and leaving a smell of ozone. The cloud shuddered, and rain started to pour down, and it washed away the accumulated dirt in the courtyard, and extinguished the fires.

Magic still hung heavily in the air. Morgan focussed her attention on the circular slab of wood over the portal. Rainbow lights skittered brightly over the surface of the ancient wood, which gleamed a shiny black. Silver and gold flecks appeared on the edge of the slab, equally spaced around the rim. A spade-like sword in a rock; a burning diamond; a heart spinning in the air; and a wand like a club the colour of the sea.

The air felt clean after the storm; Morgan slumped in the now tidy courtyard, shivering and exhausted. Nonetheless, she gave a triumphant smile.

"Spade and Earth for Art; Fire and Diamonds for Pwff; Hearts and Mysteries in the Air for Merlin; Wand across the Sea for myself. You wanted a Destiny, Art. I've given you one."

Then she grinned. "That was *fun*. What's our next adventure?" Then she fell over with exhaustion.

Afterword.
The Historical Background

As you will have worked out, the main characters in this story are taken from the legends of King Arthur.

Of course, there are many legends of King Arthur, and not all of them are consistent with each other.

Arthur was the son of Uther Pendragon and Ygraine; Uther was – according to the legends – convinced that his son would be a Great King. I have often wondered how Uther would have reacted if his first child was, in fact, a daughter and not a son.

By all accounts, King Uther was a violent and rash man. I don't think he would take the news very well.

Morgan le Fay, or le Fey, is a very complicated character. In the first legends, she's a character on the side of Good. In later legends, she's on the side of Evil. Different legends say she is Arthur's aunt, or his half-sister, or his lover, or has no real connection to him at all. You can essentially take your pick.

As for "le Fay", the Fay – or the Fey as they are more usually known – are the elves of British legend. These are not like the elves of fantasy games. These are not noble and high-minded near-humans with similar motivations. These are Fey, who do not act like humans, who are malicious and cruel. They steal babies, they lure people into their elf-hills and keep them there. They send agents into human towns and villages to cause trouble.

As a result, when some of the Arthurian legends said that Morgan was "part-Fey", I decided that she was an outcast from both cultures, and she had talents from each.

As for Merlin, the legends are even more confusing about him than they are about Morgan. He's described in different places as: a magician, an advisor, a demon, a half-demon, a druid, an acolyte of an old religion. One legend says he lives backwards in time, growing younger rather than older.

His name has been variously Merlin, Myrddin, and Talesin. In addition, Myrddin has been translated variously as "mad man" (mer dyn), "man of many names" (myrdd dyn) and "man of wonder" (marz dyn). Good luck with getting any sort of consistency with all that.

I've decided to go with a young shape-changer, someone with a lot of book learning but possibly rather less life experience. And someone who, to retain the hints of a demonic heritage, is a very argumentative person. Not aggressive, but always challenging and questioning.

Which brings us finally to Pwff. You'll search in vain to find references to Pwff in the Arthurian legends. I've invented the character. It seemed that since Arthur's name was Pendragon, which means (among other things) "with dragon", then a dragon needed to be with Art.

It couldn't be a big, fierce dragon. That would have made things too easy for Art. Besides, everyone else in the group was young, it made sense for Pwff to be young.

Which completed the group.

What comes next for the four in Art's group?

Obviously, to find out you'll have to buy the next book. What I can say is that having introduced Art, Morgan, Merlin, and the Round Table, it is very likely that we'll get to meet other members of the Arthurian legends. There's plenty to choose from.

Printed in Great Britain
by Amazon

47456757R00059